Charles Seale-Hayne Library
University of Plymouth
On   (01752) 588 588

S U R V

ONE of THE FATHER of THE SHIP INDUSTRY

Chief Steward Mr. FRANK DRUMMOND

Written in November 1997

BY FRED ELLIS

THE DAWN OF THE CRUISE INDUSTRY

Table of Contents

MY EARLY DAYS AT SEA 5

THE DAWN OF THE CRUISE INDUSTY 11

NEW NORWEGIAN CRUISE COMPANIES DISCOVER MIAMI 21

THE CRUISE BOOM CONTINUES IN THE 1970s 29

MY WIFE ELOISE 43

A BLACK MAN PAVES THE WAY IN THE CRUISE INDUSTY 47

SEARCHING FOR THE BEST CREW 51

STRIKES AND LABOR UNIONS 55

MOVING UP THE RANKS 61

MY FIRST PROMOTION 67

IN CONCLUSION 69

MY TRIBUTE TO THE LEGENDARY CHIEF STEWARD DRUMMOND 73

"fair winds and a following sea." 77

Preface 79

MY EARLY DAYS AT SEA

Chapter One:

In 1929 when I was 14 years old, I left my family in Negril, Jamaica to travel to the Capital Kingston in search of work. Barefoot and clad a shirt made from an old flour sack, I hitched a ride to Kingston on the back of a pickup truck.

After three days in Kingston where I didn't know a soul and slept on the streets, I saw something I had never seen before-a big boat called *Don Fire* docking at the Port Royal Street Wharf. From the talk on the pier, I learned that the ship had arrived to load sugar that was destined for Philadelphia.

While they were loading the cargo, I climbed on board to look around and encountered a crewmember that I learned later that he was the ship's cook. I asked him if he had any work for me. Miraculously, he replied that he was looking for someone to clean the kitchen, but needed to speak with the Captain of the ship to get his permission to hire me. After obtaining the Captain's approval, I was added to the crew list to begin my duties immediately.

As I was destitute and barefoot, the cook gave me a pair of his shoes. Although they were too big for me, I was delighted to have them since I had never owned shoes in my life. I worked from 4:00 AM to 8:00 PM every day cleaning the kitchen floor, walls, stove and dishes as well as dumping garbage and performing any other tasks that the cook assigned to me. For my efforts, I was paid $10 dollars per month. When the ship arrived in Texas, I was given my first wages, which I spend on a pair of white shoes. I worked hard to please the cook and the Captain and after six months, the Captain gave me a raise to $15 dollars per month.

For three years, I worked on the *Don Fire* while the ship carried cargo, mainly oil in five-gallon drums. On an irregular, the Don Fire visited various ports including, Philadelphia, Texas, a port close to the city of Fortaleza, a Brazilian port, including Manaus far up the Amazon River with her cargo of cans of cooking oil and kerosene for lamps. In 1933 while the ship was discharging her cargo in Norfolk, Virginia, I approached the

Captain of another ship docked there for a job. He offered me a higher salary and so I left the Don Fire for a better position onboard the *Asulite*.

The *Asulite* was a banana boat, which had just arrived from Ecuador to deliver a load of bananas to Norfolk and Philadelphia. I was hired as a mess man to serve food to the crew for $40 dollars per month. The *Asulite* traveled mainly from Costa Rica and Honduras to Philadelphia and Norfolk with cargos of bananas.

After two years on the *Asulite*, I ran into a friend on the ship Cristal that was docked alongside the *Asulite* in Philadelphia. He told me they were looking for a mess man and the salary was $75 dollars per month, an increase of $35 dollars over what I was earning on the *Asulite*. That very day in 1935, I resigned from my job on the *Asulite* and embarked on the Cristal.

The *Cristal* also transported bananas, taking crops from Ecuador, Cuba, Haiti, Honduras, Costa Rica and Texas, depending on the growing season and availability of product, to Philadelphia and other U.S. markets. After three years on the *Cristal*, I changed ships and my course in the marine industry.

THE DAWN OF THE CRUISE INDUSTY

Chapter Two:

In 1938, the *Cristal* arrived in New Orleans to unload bananas. While there, I notice a ship called the *Louis Fraizer along side of us*. This ship carried 100 passengers as well as cargo and I learned from one of their crew that the Captain was looking for a third cook. After speaking whit the Captain and applying for the job, he told me to return the next morning to join the vessel. Early the following morning, I resigned from my position on the *Cristal* and joined the Louis Fraizer.

The ship sailed from New Orleans and transported bananas and passengers from Santo Domingo,, Dominican Republic; Santa Marta, Colombia; Galveston, Texas and Haiti and to other U.S. ports. After three years on board the Louis Fraizer, I received a phone call from the owner of the ship, Mr. Frank Leslie Fraizer, who told me he needed me to come to Miami where the home office was. He then told me he wanted me to go to Boston with him to see a ship he had bought for a new company, Eastern Steamship Lines, a partnership between Fraizer and some Miami ship purveyors.

In 1941, I met Mr. Fraizer in Miami and we traveled to Boston where the ship *Yarmouth* was being readied for passenger cruise service. For two weeks, I stayed in a hotel at night and worked on the ship all day cleaning, and organizing and preparing the ship for passengers and crewmembers.

On Saturday morning, the owner presented me with a little box that he said was representative of the ship and by giving me this box, he was symbolically putting the ship into my hands.

He then instructed me to go to the airport and meet the crew that had been hired from all over the Caribbean. Work continued in Boston for a short while after the crew arrived the ship's flag was changed from American to Panamanian and the ship, capable of holding 300 crewmembers and 900 passengers, sailed from Boston to Miami. The ship stayed at the pier in Miami for one month while the finishing touches were applied and arrangements made for its inauguration into cruise service.

Eastern Steamship, owned by Mr. Frank Leslie Fraizer, was a pioneer in the modern-day cruise industry. In the early 1940s Mr.Fraizer and some of these employees developed a plan to take passengers on cruises from Miami to the Dominican Republic, Jamaica, Haiti and the Bahamas. Initially, Mr. Fraizer, I and other members of his team visited these countries and presented our operational plan to various governments. All were very receptive to having regular passenger ship calls, offering Eastern Steamship incentive and subsidies in the form of $105,000 dollars per year from the Dominican Republic, 18,000 pounds sterling(the equivalent of $72,000 dollars back then) per year from Jamaica, complimentary dockage and customs fees in Haiti and $150,000 per year from the Bahamas Government.

After gaining government support and approval in the various ports, we approached local Miami companies to assist us in bringing this plan to fruition. Operating on shoestring budget, a meeting was held with Eastern Steamship officials and representatives of Miami Grocers (called "High Hat"), food suppliers; Riverside Laundry, laundry and lines suppliers; Hopkins Carter, purveyors of marine hardware and other assorted necessary supplies; an Belcher Oil, the local fuel supplier. The meeting began in Eastern Steamship's offices at 6 PM during which time Mr. Frazer presented his plans and asked for three month credit from each of them so the ship could begin sailing and generating revenue.

Opinions and ideas were exchanged; a consensus reached at 2 AM; and the dream of operating a cruise ship came true. After these pieces were in place, the Miami Tourist Board was advised that the ship *Yarmouth* would like to call Miami home. They were proud and delighted to be the homeport for a new tourist attraction and assigned the Yarmouth permanently to Pier 2, now know as Bayside.

The Yarmouth then entered service as the first ship dedicated to cruising, rather than transportation, on 10-day cruises from Miami to Kingston, Jamaica; Santo Domingo, Dominican Republic; Port-au-Prince, Haiti; and Nassau, Bahamas. In the 1940s, cruising lacked the popularity it enjoys today and the first cruise departed in November 1940 with 10 passengers. After one year of service, the ship was sailing with 300 passengers.

My job title was supervisor of the steward department. This was an officer's position and I worked under an Italian named Mr. Max Batonia. Our department was responsible for keeping the ship's interior clean and tidy. This was a large job as it encompassed all the passenger cabins, public areas and crew areas. We also were in charge of luggage and provision loading. Fifty-three crewmembers worked for me to perform these tasks: 30 Room Stewards, 10 Cleaners, 7 Bellboys and 6 Officers' Stewards. For my work, I was paid $200 per month. As I had trouble reading and writing, I had one of my employees assist me with writing and filing my correspondence in addition to his regular duties. I worked very hard, always thinking and planning about what needed to be done and following up with my men to make sure that they carried out their assigned duties. I got along well with the Captain, crew and people that worked ashore.

In those days, crew quarters were very basic. The crew was housed in unaired-conditioned barracks-type cabins, usually eight to 12 in room.

After the United States entered World War II, the government commissioned the Yarmouth and converted her to a hospital ship. From 1942 to 1945, the ship was assigned to the Pacific arena, traveling to Hawaii and the Philippines. The crew did not mind the disruption from our regular cruise service as we received war risk pay and during the war, we would not have had many passengers on board anyway.

After four years on board, Eastern Steamship purchased a second ship in 1945. Named the *Evangeline*, the ship was purchase from Eastern Shipping and delivered to Eastern Steamship Company in Boston. Once again, I was assigned to travel to Boston to board the ship as supervisor of the steward department and d as much preparation as possible to sail from the Port of Miami. The 950 passenger Evangeline was slated for 12-day cruise from Miami to Kingston, Jamaica, Santo Domingo, St. Thomas, US Virgin Islands and San Juan, Puerto Rico. After each 12-day cruise the ship made twice-weekly cruises to Havana, Cuba, before resuming the 12-day schedule. Most of the cruise passengers were wealthy Americans who enjoyed the shows and casinos in Havana. The crew enjoyed visiting Havana as well as we were well treated by the Cubans and we could attend the shows at the Copacabana and other big casinos.

I worked on board the *Evangeline* for two years as supervisor of the steward department before my assignment to the next ship Easter Steamship purchased.

As cruising was growing in popularity and Eastern Steamship was doing well in 1949, the

company purchases a third vessel, named the
Bahamas Star, The *ex-Rose Star*, from German
American Line. After completion of the
purchase, I was assigned to the ship as
supervisor of the steward department once again
and joined the ship in Bermuda for the
repositioning voyage to Miami. The Bahamas Star
was capable of carrying 970 passengers and was
put into service on twice-weekly cruises to
Nassau from Miami. After five years on the
Bahamas Star, I was assigned to another new
Easter Steamship.

In 1954, Eastern Shipping, which continued to
prosper, purchased a fourth vessel in Germany.
Acquired from German American Lines the ship
Ariadne was more luxurious but significantly
smaller than the other ships Eastern Steamship
had bought as it only held 500 passengers. I
sailed from Germany to Miami to prepare the ship
for service on trans-Atlantic crossing. The
Ariadne was placed on a seven-day cruise
itinerary, calling in Barbados, St. Thomas, St.
Maarten, Trinidad, Tobago and Grenada.

In 1964, Mr. Louis Fraizer purchased another
vessel from an Israeli owner named the *SS Nili*.
I flew to Germany to board the ship and sail
with it to Miami. Capable of carrying 600
passengers, the *Nili* began making twice-weekly
cruises to Nassau.

I was assigned the position of Acting Chief Steward, in charge of cabin service and cleanliness of the cabins and public areas – essentially the same duties I had performed as supervisor of the steward department – and worked on board the *Nili* for six months. At this time, Eastern Steamship was facing falling revenues and in order to cut operating costs, they made a decision to sell the ship to new owners, who originally planned to keep the ship in Miami using Arison Shipping Company as operating agent, but due to some legal difficulties at the last moment took it to Israel. After the *Nili* departed, I learned from Mr. Ted Arison, who I met when he took a cruise on the *Nili*, that a Norwegian company had built a new ship that was coming to Miami. Fearful that the financial situation at Eastern Steamship would result in further reductions in their fleet, I was worried about my job when I was approached by Mr. Ted Arison to work on a brand new ship that was destined for the Miami cruise market. I resigned from Eastern Steamship and wished well by Mr. Louis Fraizer. Despite leaving this company, he, his sons and I remained very good friends.

NEW NORWEGIAN CRUISE COMPANIES DISCOVER MIAMI

Chapter Three:

A new player arrived in Miami to enter the cruise shipping industry in 1965. Two cruise industry pioneers teamed up to from Klosters Reederei, a partnership between Mr. Knut Kloster, a Norwegian Shipping Magnate and Mr. Ted Arison, owner of Arison Shipping Company. This partnership came about since Arison Shipping had the sales, marketing and management team in position in Miami to begin handling the *Nili*. As that ship was forced on short notice to return to Israel, Mr. Ted Arison was left with a company with no ship. Meanwhile, Mr. Knut Kloster had planned to send his newly built ship, the *MV Sunward*, into cruise service in Spain, but tents there precluded that possibility so they teamed up to bring the *MV Sunward* to Miami. Thus, Norwegian Caribbean Cruise Line (NCCL) now called was born.

The Sunward was docked in Bergen, Norway when I joined the ship as Chief Steward. After accepting this new position, before I left for *Norway*, I traveled to Jamaica and Nassau to recruit crewmembers to staff the steward department. I chose inexperienced seamen, promised to train them to do the required work and arrange for them to arrive in Miami when the ship arrived at that port. Upon arrival in

Miami, Mr. Knut Kloster met us as the ship docked. Also, waiting on the pier were the crew I had hired for the Steward Department.

Mr. Kloster was concern about whether the Norwegian officers on the ship would accept the black Caribbean nationals, who were going to work in the Steward Department, He expresses his concern to me but then said that the ship would only be in Miami for three months before returning to cruise in Europe. When it came to the ship leaving back to Europe, I respectfully told him I disagreed, as I knew the cruise business was lucrative in Miami, and as it happened, business was booming and the ship stayed as I had predicted.

Mr. Knut Kloster had indicated, the Norwegian officers did not like the black crew and were very resentful of us. The treated us badly and discriminated against us, including such measures as refusing to eat with us. One of my many challenges was to figure out how to feed the officers and crew in the one small mess hall available for this purpose. My solution was to create two seating – first seating was for the officers and second seating for the crew. I also convinced the Caribbean nationals that if they wanted to retain their jobs they had better cooperate with the Norwegians, no matter how poorly they felt they were being treated.

With a maximum passenger capacity of 600, the *Sunward* sailed on three and four day cruises to Nassau. I remained on board the ship for two years before NCCL assigned me to a new ship they had just constructed.

With the success of the *Sunward* in Miami market, Mr. Kloster commissioned the building of a new ship designed to carry passengers and cargo. Built in Germany, the *MV Starward* was completed in 1968. I was ordered to travel to Germany once again to join the ship on the crossing to Miami. Capable of carrying 800 passengers plus containers on her lower deck, the *Starward* undertook seven-day cruise from the Port of Miami to Port Antonio and Kingston, Jamaica and Port-au-Prince, Haiti. As with the Sunward, the ship was staffed with Norwegian deck and engine officers. The steward, food and beverage department personnel were from the Caribbean and Central American countries. I held the position of Chief Steward on this ship for three years.

In the following year NCCL added the 900 passenger ship MV Skyward to its fleet. Built in Germany, I was again asked to travel to the shipyard and start to ready the public areas for the passengers on the crossing to Miami. With the addition of the Skyward to the Miami based cruise fleet, cruising gained in popularity as the ship made seven day cruises to San Juan, Puerto Rico, St. Thomas, US Virgin Island, St. Maarten and Nassau Bahamas. Utilizing their previously successful formula, the ship was staffed by Norwegian deck and engine officers possessing excellent seamanship and friendly, outgoing Caribbean and Central America crewmembers to serve the passengers.

As on the other NCCL ships, I held the position of Chief Steward and earned $600.00 dollars per month.

Continued success in the industry caused NCCL to build yet another new ship, sister ship to the Skyward named Starward, which was delivered to the company in Italy in 1969. Following the success of NCL's *Starward* and *Skyward,* a second pair of sisters was ordered from Italian builders, to be named *Southward* in 1971 and the *Seaward.* The cost of the second ship Seaward increased following the nationalization of the builders, and the order was cancelled. In all cases I was sent as Chief Steward to break in the ship and train the crew for the pleasure of serving the American passengers. I traveled to

Italy this time and worded onboard for two years
as Chief Steward for $600 per month.

Success in the cruise industry and competition
from other lines prompted NCCL to sell the
Sunward and build new ones thus enabling them to
compete with the brand new ships of Royal
Caribbean. In the mid 1970s, the *Sunward* was
sold to Arison Shipping Company. The ship was
moved to the United Arab Emirates where it
served as a floating hotel during the Middle
East Oil Boom.

NCCL's success in developing the Miami cruise
market was not lost to Royal Caribbean Cruise
Line (RCCL), another Norwegian owned shipping
company. I approached RCCL for a job when I
learned that they were building a brand new 900
passenger vessel, named *Song of Norway*, in
Finland. Mr.Peter Whelpton, their Operations
Manager, offered me a better pay position and
hired me as Chief Steward for the salary of $800
dollars per month and I left to join the ship in
Helsinki.

After nine months on this state-of-the-art ship
that cruised for seven days to San Juan, St.
Thomas and Nassau, I was assigned to the
position of Chief Steward of another RCCL ship
Nordic Prince, also constructed in Helsinki,

Finland at Wartsila Marine Ship Yard. The ship carried 900 passengers and sailed from Miami on a 14 day itinerary to Barbados, Trinidad, San Juan, St. Thomas and Nassau.

As with NCCL, RCCL employed Norwegian deck and engine officers with the remainder of the crew a mixture of nationalities from the Caribbean and Central Americans. After a year during which I earned $800 per month, I left RCCL to join another newcomer to the Miami cruise industry.

THE CRUISE BOOM CONTINUES IN THE 1970s

Chapter Four:

One Saturday in 1972 after the *Nordic Prince* docked in Miami, I learned that Mr. Ted Arison, President of Arison Shipping Company, was arriving in Miami from New York and wanted to meet with me the next day. On Sunday afternoon, one of his executive came to pick me up to meet with him. He told me that he and NCCL had come to a parting of the ways and he was going to start his own cruise line. He asked me to come and work for him and as he had always treated me will, I listened. His charismatic personality and promises finally convinced me to leave RCCL and join his start-up venture. He went on to say that he was leaving for England the next day to look for a ship and wanted me to accompany him to give him my opinion before he made a purchase.

I accompanied him to England and with the help of a shipbroker, we spent one month looking for a suitable vessel. One Monday morning, the shipbroker advised Mr. Arison that he had located a ship in Liverpool. After a three-hour taxi ride, we arrived in Liverpool and saw a Canadian Pacific ship, the *Empress of Canada*, which had been out of operation for three years. Mr. Arison was dismayed and voiced his opinion that he couldn't buy the ship as it was very old and dilapidated and would not be able to compete with the new Miami-based RCCL and NCCL ships. I

told him that it would be a good investment,
that should buy it as it was by far the largest
ship to sail from Miami and all we had to do was
clean her, paint her and offer the passengers
superior food and entertainment. After
considering what I had said, Arison told me I
knew more about ships than he, did and he
decided to take the risk and make the purchase.
He immediately placed a call to an old friend of
his Mr. Meshulam Rikilis, who owned American
International Travel Service in Boston, who he
had previously approached to bankroll the
purchase. The check immediately arrived by
courier for deposit in Canadian-Pacific's
account and the sale proceeded. The title to
the ship was transferred and the first ship of
the fledgling Carnival Cruise Lines was renamed
Mardi Gras.

The *Mardi Gras*, which had been a multi-class
liner for Canadian Pacific, was rushed into
service as the company did not have the
operating capital to fully prepare her and
refurbish her while sitting empty at the dock.
On Saturday, March 18, 1972, a mere few days
after the arrival in Miami, she set sail on her

maiden voyage, destined for Montego Bay, St. Thomas and San Juan, and immediately ran aground I the Miami channel. She was unharmed but remained there for close to 24 hours before being freed by tug boats. Despite the inauspicious start, we slowly but surely made headway in converting and cleaning the ship, and after six months I asked Mr. Arison to invite the broker to take a cruise.

The broker and his wife traveled to Miami and had me paged when they arrived on the ship. After greetings and handshakes, he expressed his amazement in the transformation telling me that if anyone tells him I walked on water, he would believe it. He commented that I had done a much better job than they had done in England, and they thoroughly enjoyed their cruise with us.

Carnival employed Italian deck and engine officers and multi-national crew mainly from the Caribbean and Central America to staff the ship.

Gradually, the ship developed a better reputation as the *Mardi Gras* became known for its lively, friendly crew, spacious sparking clean cabins and fu atmosphere. The Italian officers treated me very well and were a pleasure to work with. I also enjoyed working for Mr. Ted Arison and Mr. Meshulam Zonis his then Vice President of Operations, who was a very visible presence on board when the ship was in Miami.

After three years, the *Mardi Gras* was sailing at full capacity week after week and Carnival Cruise Lines was shopping for another vessel to add to the fleet. In 1975, Ted Arison, Meshulam Zonis and I traveled to Piraeus, Greece to inspect a ship for sale. Owned by Greek Line and called the *Queen Anna Maria*, the ship had been built in England for Canadian Pacific Line in 1965 and had previously been called the Empress of Britain.

The ship had been laid up at anchor in Piraeus for a considerable period after Greek Line discontinued service, but all agreed that the potential was there for her to become an asset to Carnival so Arison purchased the ship and named her *Carnivale*. I was appointed Chief Steward and for $800 per month, I had the responsibility of cleaning and organizing another old vessel. Again, time was an issue and we worked day and night from the moment the contract was signed in December 1975 until the inaugural cruise on February 7, 1976 when the ship made her maiden voyage to San Juan, St. Thomas and St. Maarten.

The *Carnivale* enjoyed immediate success as we brought the ship up to the standards of the *Mardi Gras* and Mr. Ted Arison started shopping for another ship just over a year after the *Carnivale* entered service. This time, he discovered a ship that was virtually unknown and far larger than the *Mardi Gras* and *Canivale*. The *S.S. Vaal* previously known as the *Transvaal Castle* was owned by Union Castle Steamship Line and operated by Safmarine, S.A. Carry passengers and cargo between Southampton and Durban and Cape Town, South Africa.

As jets had become the preferred means of long distance travel, revenue had dropped off considerably and the ship was for sale.

Arison was impressed with the ships potential and negotiated to add it to the *Carnival* fleet. The sale was consummated in late 1977 and the ship changed hands. Carnival was finally in a financial position to convert the cargo spaces on the ship and overhaul the vessel before beginning cruise service. A conversion contract was negotiated with Kawasaki Heavy Industries and the ship, renamed *Festivale*, set sail for Kobe, Japan where it remained for eight months evolving into a one class ship with a capacity of 1400 passengers, a capacity that far exceeded any other Miami based cruise ship.

I journeyed to Japan on the ship and had a chance to visit Tokyo, which I was most impressed with. After the conversion, the ship sailed across the Pacific Ocean and on to Miami via the Panama Canal. On October 28, 1978, the TSS Festivale began cruise service on seven-day cruises to San Juan, St. Thomas and St. Maarten.

Not content to rest on his laurels and desiring a brand new ship specifically tailored to "Fun Ship" image Carnival had cultivated and the desires of the American cruising public, Arison made a daring move in a time of rising fuel prices and suppressed economy. He commissioned a new ship to build by Aalborg Vaerft in Aalborg, Denmark.

Slated for completion in late 1981. I was assigned to the new ship as Chief Steward. When the ship neared completion; I traveled to Denmark for familiarization and supervision of the finishing touches. After arrival of the bulk of the crew and ceremony delivering the ship to Carnival and naming her *Tropicale*, we set sail for Miami. As the ship crossed the Atlantic Ocean, my crew and I readied the cabins and public spaces for a multitude of inaugural festivities in Miami.

On January 16, 1982 after a week of gala events and parties in Miami, the ship, named *Troicale*, commenced cruise service on a seven-day run from Miami to Cozumel, Mexico, Grand Cayman and Ocho Rios, Jamaica. The ship spent the winter months on the western Caribbean run before transiting the Panama Canal on the way to Vancouver for cruise to Alaska during the summer months. Following the Alaska season, the Tropicale took up residence in Los Angeles for seven-day cruises to the Mexican Rivera.

In 1984, I joined Paquet Cruises, a new entrée vessel destine for the Miami Cruise Market, call the *ss Rhapsody*, which they had just purchased. A French company, Paquet Cruises had purchase the SS Statendam from Holland American Line and opened an office in Miami with the intention of expanding their cruise operation to the Miami market.

We met the ship at Norfolk Shipbuilding and Dry-dock Company in Norfolk Virginia where the ship was being inspected and machinery readied for service. During the voyage from Norfolk to Miami, my crew and I worked extremely hard to ready the public areas and cabins.

For my efforts, Mr. William Shanz, the president of the company gave me a $400 per month increase in pay, increasing my wages as Chief Steward to $1,200 dollars per month.

With French officers and a multi-national service crew, the ship sailed on seven-day cruises from Miami to Ocho Rios, Jamaica, Grand Cayman and Cozumel Mexico. My crew and I enjoyed working with the French officers but after a year, Paquet Cruise sold the ship and left the American market so I began working for another company.

Owned by Sundance Cruise – new company founded by Mr. Stanley MacDonald, a Seattle entrepreneur who was the founder of Princess Cruises – the 600 passenger Sundance was purchased from a Swiss corporation and dock in Sweden when I joined the ship in 1986. As Chief Steward, my wages were $1,500 per month.

After crossing the Atlantic and stopping in Miami for Fuel and provisions, the ship continued through the Panama Canal to its ultimate destination, Vancouver, Canada. The ship then spent the summer sailing on seven-day cruises from Vancouver along the Inside Passage to Alaska ports. On one cruise while in Alaskan waters, the Sundance hit a submerged object and ruptured her hull. The captain quickly grounded the ship on a rock. The aft section was partially submerged to just above the engine room. I assisted in evacuating first the passengers and then the crew. Fortunately, there were no casualties.

After nine months on the *Sundancer*, I was assigned to the company's newly acquired ship named Stardancer. I traveled to Denmark to join the ship. We journeyed to Miami and then through the Panama Canal and up the West Coast to her homeport of Vancouver in the Summer time with cruise to Alaska, and the homeport in Los Angeles in the Winter with cruise to Mexico all of them on day cruises. The Stardancer cruised on seven-day voyages to Puerto Vallarta, Manzanillo and Acapulco. For two years, I served as Chief Steward and was paid $1,700 per month.

In 1989, I became associated with Premier Cruise Lines. The newly formed company purchased the

Oceanic from the now-defunct Home Lines and renamed the ship the *Starship Oceanic*. The ship affectionately became known to the public as *"The Big Red Boat"* due to its distinctive red hull that was painted after the sale from Home Lines. I joined the ship in New York as Chief Steward for the salary of $2000 per month.

The *SS Oceanic* was based in Port Canaveral, Florida and made three and four day trips to the Bahamas in conjunction with Disney World vacations. The success of this concept and popularity of the *SS Oceanic* resulted in rapid growth for Premier over the course of the next five years. A second ex-Home line vessel, the Starship Atlantic, which was laid up in Germany, was purchased and I was transferred to that ship to ready it on the Trans Atlantic crossing. The *SS Atlantic* also cruised from Port Canaveral on three and four day trips to the Bahamas.

My final Premier Cruise Lines ship was the SS Majestic, which was purchased in Germany. Once again, I was given the position of Chief Steward and sailed on the ships its traveled from Europe to Port Canaveral to commence three and four day cruises to the Bahamas.

After five years employment with Premier on
March 9, 1994 I joined the American Adventure, a
cruise ship with American owners. I was however
paid by Stellar Maritime and World Wide Co, they
were the caters of the ship. As Chief Steward
with a salary of $2,500 per month, I joined the
ship in Italy for the crossing to Miami. The
American Adventure then made 15-day cruises from
Miami to Nassau, Santo Domingo, San Blas,
Barbados, St. Maarten, St. Thomas and San Juan.

After ten months, the ship was sold and left
Miami for Singapore. I returned to Premier
Cruise Lines where I worked until 1994.

Following my second stint with Premier, I was
hired as Executive Chief Steward with Discovery
Cruise in 1995. I worked aboard both of their
vessels, *Discovery I* and *Discovery Sun*.
Discovery I made day cruises from Ft. Lauderdale
to Freeport and short cruises to nowhere.
Discovery Sun sailed on the same itinerary from
Miami. Her Christening and inaugural cruise was
March 1995. I board her *"Discovery Sun"* 1997.
The *Discovery I*, was taken out of service and

replace by *Discovery Dawn* at the end of 1996.
As Executive Chief Steward I was required to
visit and inspect all ships in the fleet.

On October 27, 1997 when this was written, I was
on board the *Discovery Sun.*

MY WIFE ELOISE DRUMMOND

Chapter Five:

In 1954 while I was working for Eastern Shipping Company, I met Eloise. She was living in New York and had traveled to Miami to visit a friend while on vacation from her job at the Bell Telephone Company. We met at a party of mutual acquaintance where we had a pleasant conversation that began our friendship.

After Eloise returned to New York, we continued our friendship through correspondence until she made the decision to move to Miami. She got a job at Flagler Federal Bank and we decided to purchase a home in Miami. We did not make much money but we were able to put together enough to buy a Ford Mustang for our transportation.

Eloise was very frugal and saved her money. On her first vacation from Flagler Federal Bank, she took a 21 day tour of Europe. When she returned, she began saving again and encourage me to put my money in the bank which I did.

After her next vacation trip to the Hawaiian Islands, she told me that our bank accounts were growing steadily and we had saved a fair amount of money. I was surprised to see how well we were doing. We saved as much as we could and paid off our home gradually over the course of 30 years.

A BLACK MAN PAVES THE WAY IN THE CRUISE INDUSTY

Chapter Six:

My Career in the cruise industry spanned close
to 55 years from the 1940's to mid-1990s.
Throughout these years, I dedicated myself to my
job and dealt honestly and fairly with all of
the companies I worked for. However, I was not
always treated honestly and fairly by most of
them. At times, I had a very hard road to
travel. I do feel whoever that there have been
one or two individuals that just forgot about
the effort and had dedicated work that I and
other rendered to them. I feel therefore, that
no man and I mean no man should ever exploit a
man's labor; it is just like a man who robs a
bank. Mean man hid it as oh well its business.
There were times that I made a gain, I was
pushed back. Sometimes I did not believe I
would be able to raise my head from the last
ordeal. I never asked for a pay raise, so when
the opportunity came knocking, I had to leave
for a better pay position.

Enough negative, back to work.

The first cruise company I worked for in the
194s and 1950s was Eastern Steamship Company. I
was on board each of their five ships on their
inaugural cruises, and I always felt that they
treated me fairly.

I joined Norwegian Caribbean Cruise Line (NCCL) now know as (NCL) in the late 1950s and remained with them through most of the 1960s as they introduced four ships to the Miami market. The owner, Knut Kloster and Operations Manager Mr. Nielson, were gentlemen, treating me fairly and me in many ways. This company was the first to give me the title of Chief Steward and define the functions and responsibilities of my job.

After NCCL, I worked Royal Caribbean Cruise Line and Carnival Cruise Line in the 1970 and early 1980s. During that time, I sailed on the inaugural cruise of two RCCL ships and four Carnival Ships. Carnival treated me with respect, and for that I am very appreciative.

From the mid-1998s to the mid-1990s, I worked for Paquet Cruises, Sundance Cruises, American Adventure and Premier Cruise Lines and all of them treated me fairly. When I was working for Discovery Cruise Lines in the mid-1990s, I was treated like a gentleman by the owner, Rafael Ordonez; President and Chief Executive Officer Martin A. Salzedo; and Director of Operations Manuel Diaz. These young men treated me better than anyone else I have met in the cruise industry. They have an excellent reputation and rapport with all of their officers and crewmembers.

SEARCHING FOR THE BEST CREW

Chapter Seven:

When Eastern Steamship Company was in its infancy, finding crewmembers that could provide good service on board was a challenge. Good help is hard to find particularly when you have to overcome language barriers, attitudes and different cultural background to deal with and manage. The company's executives decided to look for suitable employees in the Caribbean where they could find people who spoke English, needed jobs and were willing to work for low wages.

We chose Jamaica to begin our search and visited the best hotels on the island. We stayed at each hotel so we could personally experience the service given to the guests. After staying in and dining at these hotels, we were able to determine who gave the best service in the dining room, prepared the best food and kept the rooms and public spaces the cleanest. We than offered those contracts to the cream of the crop.

Our policy in order to save on airfare was never to hire a worker from the Caribbean unless the ship called in his country so we had crewmembers from Jamaica, the Dominican Republic, Haiti and Cuba. The best workers were from Cuba and Jamaica.

As the years have gone by, the cruise industry expanded and changed rapidly. When it was just a case of staffing five ships, it was easy to find plenty of honest, dedicated workers. Today, it is much more difficult to find suitable crewmembers and the industry has been forced to compromise. Now we have all types of officers and crew, some of who are disrespectful, undisciplined and lacking in pride.

When a man loses his pride, he loses everything. The whole world has changed and we have to go with the flow but not a night passes that I knot go to bed think about what has become of the cruise industry. They have changed everything to suit themselves. Some have little or no respect for their company's well being and survivorship. To miss quote a little bit of a Famous American President saying " ask not what the cruise company can do for you, but what you the crew can do for the betterment of your ship", which is your bread and butter and don't ever forget that.

STRIKES AND LABOR UNIONS

Chapter Eight:

Eastern's labor troubles were not over as the Yarmouth became the target of labor union. One Saturday evening in Baltimore at the start of a seven-day cruise to Bermuda with 900 passengers on board, six buses arrived at the dock one half hour before sailing. Some men got off the buses and asked to see the captain. We took them to the captain and learned afterwards that they were representatives of the National Maritime Union in Baltimore.

They had arrived to enroll the crew as union members so they could be paid union wages. The

When Eastern Steamship purchased the *Ariadne* in Germany in 1952, they sailed to England, changed to a British flag and replaced the Germans with an English crew. I was the only black man from the Caribbean employed on board.

The ship made her inaugural cruise from Miami and arrived in Barbados on New Year's Day. At lunchtime, the waiters and cabin stewards went on strike because they wanted to go ashore and the captain wouldn't let them. Lunch was served to the passengers by other crewmembers including myself as Supervisor, the ship's doctor, cleaners and bellboys. The waiter and cabin stewards returned to their duties before dinner and the ship proceeded to continue the cruise and return to Miami.

Upon arrival in Miami, the company fired and repatriated all of the English crewmembers and the ship was laid up. I was assigned to one of the other Eastern Steamship vessels at that time. Six month later, a new crew from the Caribbean was hired. The company changed the ship's flag from British to Liberian and began cruises again.

Captain explained he would have to consult with the Miami office before allowing them to talk to the crew and after doing so, informed them that the office had refused to grant them permission. The union replied that if they were refusing, they would ask the crew to get off the ship and go with them to the union hall. The majority of the crew decided to go with them. The company cancelled the cruise, put the passenger in hotels and brought the ship to Miami with 25 crewmembers on board.

After three days, the ship reached Miami and the crew, who had disembarked in Baltimore, was sent to Miami by bus. The company allowed them to board the ship under police escort to collect their belongings before sending them back to their homeland.

The ship was then laid up in Jacksonville. After six months, new crewmembers from the Caribbean arrived and cruises began again. The union, however, did not give up. They continued to harass Eastern Steamship, demanding that an election be held among the crewmembers so they could decide for themselves whether to join the union. We asked the company to relent and agree to hold an election in one month. During that month, I had meetings with the crew where AI explained exactly what had happened to the previous crew, telling them that company did not want the union and that the ship

had been tied up for six months and everyone had lost their jobs. After explaining the situation to them, I asked them whether they wanted the union and almost everyone was in agreement that they did not want to belong to the union.

After the month had passed, I went to the office and told them to call the union representative and tell them we were ready for the election. Six representatives arrived from Baltimore. The ship docked early on Thursday morning. The passengers debarked and we cleaned and readied the ship for the cruise. The election began and everyone except one crewmember from Grand Cayman, voted against the union. I took the news to the office told the owner we had won the election. He thanked me profusely saying he couldn't give me money but only thanks from the bottom of his heart. He went on to say that if the union had won the election we would have had no choice but to unionize all the five ships in the fleet. The ship began flying the Panamanian flag. The president of the union approached me and told me I was the most marvelous man he had ever encountered and I was a good fighter.

These are just a couple of the problems we encountered in the early days of the cruise industry. I was the one who saved the shipping industry in Miami, Florida. Today there are people from all over the world working in the cruise industry. You hear the names of lots of countries but you don't hear about the Caribbean countries that are the ones who built the cruise industry.

MOVING UP THE RANKS

Chapter Nine:

At every company I worked for, I gave my crew a chance to work hard and move up to a more responsible, better paying position. I taught them everything I know thus qualifying them for the position of Chief Steward. Many of the gentlemen listed below have worked for several companies in the industry, proof of their capabilities and knowledge glean under my tutelage.

Rafael Ordonez – Hired as Bell Boy. Now owner and president of Apollo Ship Chandler and Discovery Cruise Lines.

Roy Hardy – Hired as Hotel Cleaner, promoted to Bellboy, then to Chief Steward.

Noel White – Hired as Hotel Cleaner, promoted to Cabin Steward, then to Chief Steward.

Manly Wilson – Hired as Hotel Cleaner, promoted to Cabin Steward, then to Chief Steward.

Miguel Sauzo – Hired as Hotel Cleaner, promoted to Cabin Steward, then to Chief Steward.

Ricardo Shaw – Hired as Hotel Cleaner, promoted to Chief Steward.

Mr. Brooks – Hired as Hotel Cleaner, promoted to Chief Steward.

Edward Frankly – Hired as Hotel Cleaner, promoted to Cabin Steward, then to Chief Steward.

Levy Wilson Hired as Linen keeper, promoted to Chief Steward.

Edgar Richardson – Hired as Linen keeper, promoted to Chief Steward.

Roderick Smith – Hired as Assistant Linen keeper, promoted to Chief Steward.

Frank McDugal – Hired as Linen keeper, promoted to Chief Steward.

Alva Ellis - Hired as Bellboy, promoted to Cabin Steward, then Chief Steward.

Garnet Lam - Hired as Bellboy, promoted to Chief Steward.

Jimmy Fagan - Hires as Bellboy, promoted to Cabin Steward, then to Chief Steward.

Mr. Barry - Hired as Bellboy, promoted to Chief Steward.

John Davos - Hired as Bellboy, promoted to Chief Steward.

Dane Bryan - Hired as Bellboy, promoted to Cabin Steward, then to Chief Steward.

Bobby Walters - Hired as Bellboy, promoted to Cabin Steward, then to Chief Steward.

Mr. Silber - Hired as Bellboy, promoted to Cabin Steward, then to Chief Steward.

Lee Wong - Hired as Bellboy, promoted to Cabin Steward, then to Chief Steward.

Peter Kovnick - Hired as Assistant Chief Steward, promoted to Chief Steward.

Wesley Samuels - Hired as Cabin Steward, promoted to Chief Steward.

MY FIRST PROMOTION

Chapter Ten:

I got my first promotion when I was with Eastern Steamship Company. The port steward, Mr. Honeycutt, called a meeting and told everyone that we were all doing our job well, but there is someone who does it best. He then called my name and told everyone that I was being promoted to the position of Third Steward. He went on to say that contrary to my education and color, I was the best worker in the department and the company was completely satisfied with my performance. The tailor measured me for my white officer's uniform. I was so proud to receive it. After putting it on, I walked around the ship looking everything over and deciding what work had to be done.

Three months later, I was promoted to Second Steward and the eight months after that to Chief Steward. I never turned back. I continued until today, and although it was often a difficult journey, I made it. I was like a tree planted by a stream whose leaves do not wither. If we are rooted Christ, there is never a drought and the tree is never malnourished. Those who are not rooted in the Lord are like cut flowers – doomed to perish as soon as they are cut from their stem. I was nourished by the grace of the Lord, and through His word, I am fulfilled.

IN CONCLUSION

Chapter Eleven:

I left my home so many years ago looking for life without knowing where I was going. My parents knew I left but the did not know where I went or what became of me.

It was difficult for me to make my way along the narrow road of honesty. Life is not always fair, but I learned not to despair because of my strong belief that the Lord of Glory is in control and our ultimate victory rests with him. Every step I took, a door opened for me.

My path in life took me to the sea. It was my destiny-a one-way path without a return. It was hard for me to continue knowing each day I was moving further and further away from home searching for a better life. It was difficult to go back home while at sea, continually moving from ship to another in search of a better position and income.

Years later, I had an opportunity to return to Kingston to look for crewmembers. At that time, I was working for Eastern Steamship Company. I was overjoyed to be returning after so many years without communication with my parents but learned they passed away without knowing what had become of me.

I found my life on the sea but it was very difficult for me to realize that I was not able to help my parents the way I wanted to. Through their sacrifices, I am here today. They gave me the best thing they could - LIFE.

MY TRIBUTE TO THE LEGENDARY CHIEF STEWARD DRUMMOND

Chapter Twelve:

I first meet Chief Steward Frank Drummond on the companion way on Upper Deck on board the TSS Mardi Gras sometime in mid 1972. I can still hear his raspy strong British Jamaican voice giving orders to a Hotel Cleaner, as to how he wanted that floor polish and clean.

He always greeted the ladies passenger with a big "Good Day Mi Lady or Good Evening Mi Lady" and to the gentleman "Good Day Sir" depending on the time of day.

Throughout my career in the cruise industry I had the honor and privilege to have worked with the Legendary Chief Steward Frank Drummond, in three different cruise lines (Carnival, Paquet French Cruises and Discovery). He was an expert in startup and inaugural cruise of many ships in the United States. If he was on board, you knew that you didn't have to worry about anything in the steward department. He was never a negative individual, on the contrary, there was nothing he couldn't tackle or was afraid to do when asked.

In all the many years that we work together, I never heard him ask for a pay raise and more interesting, he never requested to see a doctor.

He never requested a dime from his cruise company nor did he ask for any type of compensation. Chief Drummond didn't believe in burden the company; on the contrary, he was always looking into saving the cruise company money and instilling that attitude in his crew. In the early days of Carnival, he knew the company was struggling and therefore he would somehow purchase the braso, a liquid to shine all the brass railings on the ship and also shoe polish, so that the cabin steward could shine their passengers' shoes.

On one of my startup / dry-dock ships that I was working and which Mr. Drummond was not on at the time with me, some divine intervention occurred. The Ship's Captain had to dismiss the acting chief steward, due to an infraction that the acting chief steward committed.

I didn't know what to do without a Chief Steward, as I was on the ship in Norfolk and not in the office and we needed urgently a replacement. The next day after the firing, I was in the Hotel Mangers office when the phone ranged out of the blue the hotel manager tells me that the phone call was for me. It was Chief Steward Frank Drummond telling me he was available for duty. I was shock, as I knew he was working for another cruise line at the time and told him that he would need to ask permission from his present Vice President of Operation to allow him to leave them and come over with us. The next day, he called me back and said they had granted that request and we sent him an airline ticket right away to join our ship.

On his arrival I had to introduce him to the hotel department crew that was meanly composed of Indonesian and Philippines and I was told by the hotel manager that they; the Indonesian and Philippines crew would not obey orders from a Black Man. To my delight and dismay, after Chief Drummond spoke to 30 some crewmembers, they gave him a standing ovation with many applauses, after he told them that he was going to teach them how to please and pamper the American Passenger in order to receive large tips. So much for those rumors, Thank God.

In another cruise line, in a much early times, there was a crew strike in the fleet of three ships at that time. But because of Chief Drummond not one of his crew members struck or made any troubled of any kind. He was their mentor and Father and they were not going to let him down.

I have lost count as to how many new startup and inaugurations that Chief Steward Mr. Frank Drummond accomplishes in his career with such easy and professionalism. I believe it is more than two dozen ships. In my book, he was a Legend in his own time and any cruise executive that had him serving on their ships was a very fortunate person.

Chief Drummond, I truly miss you and may your legend endure, as many people owe you many thanks, praise and gratitude, including myself. God Bless you and your wife Eloise.

Chief Drummond was a Gentleman, an Officer and a Legend in his Own Right and Time.

We will all miss you Chief, God Bless you......... Martin A. Salzedo.

"fair winds and a following sea."

The traditional farewell (or toast) of a mariner is wishing a friend "fair winds and following seas." The full version is **"Fair winds and following seas and long may your big jib draw!"** The phrase may also be considered a Naval blessing as well as a farewell. "We bid shipmates farewell with this naval blessing because it represents the ideal underway conditions for which Sailors yearn." It is also said for a departed mariner at a funeral.

Dear Chief Frank Drummond; May you experience "Fair Winds and a Following Sea" where ever you may be in Heaven.

In another quotation to honor Mr. Drummond is:

To re-arrange a quote from General Douglas McArthur: "Old Seafarers never die, they just fade away".

Chief Drummond and Captain at the Captains Gala Party on board

Preface

This book is the auto biography of Chief Steward Frank Drummond. He relates his years at sea, at the dawn of the cruise industry in the South Florida the Cruise Capital of the World.

He gives you his prospective of how a young 14 year old barefooted black man makes an impact in the early days of the cruise industry, through to the modernization of the industry that he loved and cherishes.

This is a must read for any cruise historian and any person involved in the cruise industry, from ship owners, managers, maritime vendors and crewmembers, to give you a bird eye view of the initial planers, visionary and determine crewmembers that help promoted and establish a new and vibrant industry in this country that helps employee tens of thousands of U.S. people and produce millions if not billions of dollars for the U.S. economy.

He shows you how a black person struggled and succeeded in this industry and gave the Caribbean and Latin America crew a chance for a better living. By showing them how to please and pamper the American public and therefore receive monetary remuneration for these exemplary services which the Caribbean and Latin America is known for with their charm and smile.

Many ship owners are mention here as well, as lots of crewmembers that he taught and help guide them to promotion and prosperity. There are many cruise lines beginning and ending and how they evolved and competed in this industry.

CPSIA information can be obtained at www.ICGtesting.com
Printed in the USA
LVOW111653100512

281228LV00011B/100/P